SCRIPTS
Of the World

written by

suzanne bukiet

illustrated by

hélène muller

&

christian lai cong phuoc

Multi-Cultural Books & Videos, Inc.
AIMS International Books, Inc.

To Christian

But let us return to the cradle of signs, to the birthplace of writing, to those clay tablets found in the palaces of Akkad and Sumer. A message was conveyed by carving into a tablet of fresh clay, putting that into the kiln where it hardened and the writing remained.

From then on, meaning was imprisoned in the clay. It became a stroke, a line, a curve or an angle; a furrow ploughed into the baked earth; the cutting point of meaning. At the beginning of history, man armed with his stylus was a labourer of sounds, a sower of signs, the noble act of the first scribe.

JACQUES LACARRIÈRE
Extract from the ''Surats''
Éditions Fayard

CONTENTS

the first words...

Knowledge, ideas and dreams were first passed from person to person and from generation to generation through words. This is known as oral culture — one that is often lively and rich.

The invention of writing marked a turning point in the development of civilisations. Writings, documents and books now form the memory of mankind. They allow each generation to progress through learning, building on the discoveries and experiences of those before them, while reducing the risk of loss or distortion of facts.

This book offers a glimpse at how writing came to be invented and the various forms it has taken throughout history and in different parts of the world.

Whilst care has been taken to be as accurate as possible, historically and geographically, the dates set in very early times should be used as a rough guide only. Similarly, the map on pages 24 and 25 shows the areas where the five main "families" of contemporary writing are to be found but without precise geographical limits.

Like all things human, writings evolve; some advance and others fall back or disappear completely only to be replaced by those of more dominant civilisations.

before...

The following story happened a very, very long time ago, when the lands that are deserts today were crossed with rivers and inhabited by all kinds of animals.

One day, a little boy called Ajjar was watching over a herd of cattle, with his tame antelope. Suddenly he spotted in the distance a family of giraffes.

In those days the giraffe was thought to be a great delicacy, and any huntsman who was clever enough to catch one was given a great feast in his honour. The men would gather together and carry the giraffe back to camp while the women prepared a huge banquet. There was eating, singing and dancing far into the night!

More than anything, Ajjar wanted to kill a giraffe. Not only because he loved the feasting but because he thought that he would then sometimes be allowed to go with the huntsmen on their expeditions. So far his father had always refused to let him.

Then, as luck would have it, Ajjar discovered that for the first time ever, he had forgotten his bow and arrows. He was a long way from the camp and dared not leave the cattle that were in his care to go and fetch his weapons.

It was at this moment that a brilliant idea came to him. He had often watched one of the men in his tribe drawing animals and hunters on the walls of the caves where they lived. Ajjar had often tried to copy him and sometimes he managed quite well... Now, he bent down and quickly took off one of the pieces of sheepskin that he wore wrapped around his feet. Taking a bit of charred wood, he began to draw on the skin.

In the bottom right hand corner he drew a herd of cattle. In the top left hand corner he drew two giraffes, and in the middle a small figure shooting with a bow and arrow. He repeated this figure several times, showing lots of arrows, so that his mother, to whom he would send this message, would understand that he needed his bow and arrows to be sent without delay!

Ajjar then tied the sheepskin to his antelope's horns, hoping that his mother would tie his favourite bow and bag of arrows in the same place. He whispered his instructions to the antelope, and sat back to wait.

The antelope set off with a leap and a bound and soon arrived in front of Ajjar's mother who was quietly cooking outside their cave. She recognised Ajjar's sheepskin with a mixture of surprise and unease. At first she could not make anything of the drawing and then suddenly she began to weep and wail so loudly that in a moment the whole tribe had gathered round her.

The poor woman was completely distraught. Waving the sheepskin in the air she sobbed that Ajjar had met with a terrible accident. He had been attacked by giraffe hunters who were trying to capture the herd of cattle, and wounded by all their arrows.

The chief of the tribe came forward slowly, as expected of a chief, and studied the drawing for a long time. Finally he agreed that Ajjar's mother had interpreted the message correctly. In seconds, all the able-bodied men had grabbed their weapons and raced off to the pasture lands.

12

You can imagine the surprise and terror of Ajjar when he saw the men from his tribe advancing on him from all directions, brandishing their weapons in a state of high excitement.

The chief, realising that Ajjar was clearly in no danger, planted himself menacingly in front of the boy, and without saying a word, handed him the sheepskin. Still trembling with fright, Ajjar then explained the meaning of his drawing.

Once the huntsmen had got over their initial surprise, they burst out laughing until the tears rolled down their cheeks. It was some time before they were able to return to the hunt again, leaving poor Ajjar, overcome with embarrassment, on his own.

This was how the first hand-drawn message came into being, but, as was to happen many times in the future, it was wrongly interpreted. Ajjar thought about it afterwards. He was annoyed in the first place as he had not been taken seriously, but perhaps more so because he hadn't managed to make himself understood. He then realised that it was very important for man to invent a system for communicating thoughts and ideas that was not open to misinterpretation.

Because so many men were preoccupied by this same idea, they finally succeeded in inventing writing. And since then, they have been trying to perfect the art of writing in an effort to make it still more precise and more faithful to the ideas it is trying to express.

On the following pages you can see the paths to their success.

These pictures are based on 3,000 years old cave drawings in the Sahara.

the birth of handwriting

Writing has not always existed...

For thousands of years our far-off ancestors communicated with each other by speech, gesture, music and even dancing.

Peoples that had no means of writing still, however, knew how to send messages. For example, the Scythes, a Nordic race from the frontiers of Europe and Asia once sent to Darius, the King of the Persians, a bird, a mouse, a frog and five arrows. The meaning of the message was:

"If you escape from us like a bird through the air, like a mouse under the ground or a frog in the water, our arrows will still kill you!"

A somewhat complicated affair!

Fortunately, as we have seen, men understood early on that they could draw. (Their drawings were often connected with magic rites.) It was through the association of small drawings, which were gradually simplified, that writing came into being, probably, it is believed, some 5,000 years ago*. Several centuries later, about 3,500 years ago*, the first alphabet was formed and from then on man has lived in a civilisation of the written word.

Sumerian tablet more than 4,000 years old. (Louvre Museum).

Pictogram from the Indians of the Cuna tribe in Panama.

* The figures given here are approximate. They are given only to help place the evolution of writing in time.

14

Gradually, the way people live has been determined by written laws. In the business world, verbal agreements have now been replaced by written contracts. Religious works based on Sacred Books have been written down to take the place of the oral tradition.

Testimonies to the lives of men who lived before the written word (such as monuments, objects and drawings), like Ajjar's story, belong to pre-historic times. The history you learn at school is based in texts and therefore begins with the written word.

Just over 5,000 years ago the SUMERIANS, a people who lived in the southern part of a country known as Mesopotamia — and today called Iraq — invented the first known handwriting.

Sumerian writing, 5,000 years old.

Each sign of the early forms of writing corresponded to a word or idea. But there were an enormous number of them which made the use of writing difficult and complicated. This was particularly so in the case of ancient Egyptian writing known as hieroglyphics which came into existence about 4,500 years ago, and Chinese writing also called ideograms or picture symbols which appeared at about the same time.

On the right : Egyptian hieroglyphics.

Chinese pictogram.

Handwriting based on drawings, known to specialists as pictograms, resemble to some extent the picture-puzzles you can enjoy trying to decipher today.

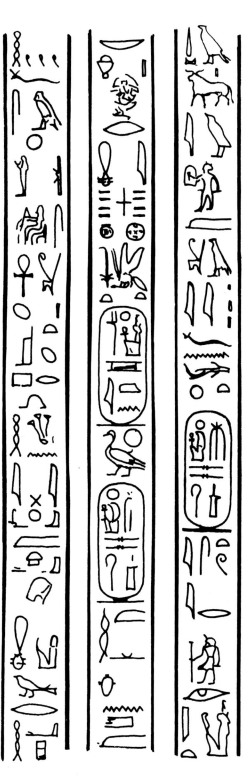

In an effort to reduce the number of necessary signs, people thought of making them correspond to sounds rather than words. As the same sound is repeated in different words the number of signs needed was reduced proportionately and writing gradually became a reflection of the spoken word.

Cuneiform (wedge-shaped) writing.

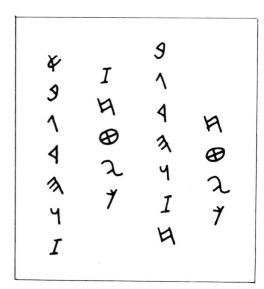

Phoenician alphabet.

Detail of the Phaestus discus, found in Crete, 1,500 B.C. It is made on clay. The text is written following a spiral pattern.

At a much later and far more advanced stage in the development of writing sounds came to be designated into letters and thus make up the alphabetic writing that we know today. It was the PHOENICIANS, who lived on the shores of the Mediterranean, where Lebanon is today, who created the first alphabet about 3,500 years ago. This was the fore runner of all the alphabets known to this day, but it was formed only of consonants.

The evolution of writing took place very slowly through a long process of trial and error. In moving further away from the "drawing" and closer to abstract signs, it then became a much simpler means of communication between people and more adaptable to the various languages it was eventually to transcribe.

The formation of writing depends to a great extent on the materials on which it is based and the instruments used. On a firm and rigid base, such as stone or wood, writing is square and geometrical in shape. But where the writing material is more supple, such as paper or parchment, the paint or brush can glide over the surface and the writing has a free and easy form.

Throughout history, men have used all kinds of basic materials on which to write — stone, bronze, bone, tortoiseshell, woodbark, silk and wax — but the finest writing surfaces have always been papyrus, paper and parchment.

Papyrus, made from the outer leaves, was very commonly used by the Egyptians, and remained in use until the 11th century.

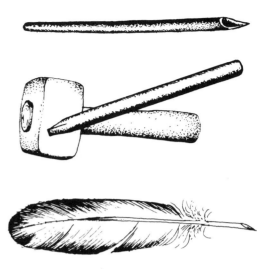

Paper, which had been made in China out of vegetable fibres for two thousand years, was introduced into Europe by the Arabs in the 12th century. Their civilisations had developed far ahead of any others and they had been making paper at Damascus and Tripoli for over five centuries.

Parchment, made from animal skin, was used until the 15th century. The strength and quality of the parchment made it preferable to paper which was considered too fragile.

The instruments used for writing have evolved in accordance with the type of writing surface being used. They have included the calam, or sharpened reed; the chisel for carving stone; the sharpened split-pointed feather; the brush, the metal pen and the ball-pen. Very early on, the Chinese made ink with soot, but chalk, coal and graphite were also used.

The invention of printing, first by the Chinese in the 7th century and then by Gutenberg in the 15th century, replaced much manual writing by mechanical methods. From then on, instead of being slowly written and copied by hand, books could be produced rapidly in multiple copies. This revolution had enormous consequences for the transmission of information and knowledge and also gave rise to the growth and the progress of democracy that we know today.

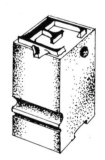

Printing character block.

This is a very simplified history of writing — itself the result of many thousands of years of research which still goes on. Over the course of time many forms of writing had been abandoned, either because they were too complex or because the civilisation to which they belonged ceased to flourish.

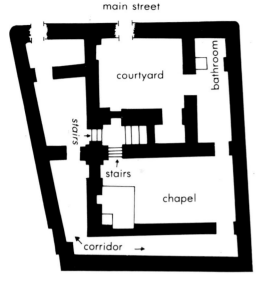

A plan of a house converted into a school in Ur, 3,800 years ago.

Tablet with cuneiform text and its envelope. Each tablet has some information on the spine so it can be filed on a shelf.

schools... and libraries

Once forms of writing had been invented, people had to be taught to read and write and it became necessary to open schools and establish libraries to preserve manuscripts.

In the ancient city of UR (in the southern part of the country known today as Iraq) a house has been discovered which was used as a school nearly 4,000 years ago. It was a small school for about 24 pupils who were taught to read and write and learned mathematics and the various sciences current at the time.

The pupils wrote on damp clay tablets with a stiletto (a thin stick of wood with a pointed end). The tablets considered worth keeping were baked in an oven and placed on shelves.

The school had a headmaster and several teachers. Schooling lasted a long time — from childhood until adulthood. After an apprenticeship of two years the pupil was put in charge of a new pupil and acted as his tutor. Discipline was very strict and pupils were "kept in" or even beaten if they were late for school or didn't work hard enough.

This is a text found on one of the tablets at the school.

"What did you do at school?"

18

"I recited the lessons on my tablet. I wrote it down and finished it. Then I was given my homework to do. When school was over I went home and found my father sitting in the house. I told him what homework I had to do and I recited my tablet to him and he was pleased."

Elsewhere, in the northern part of Iraq, at the TELL HARMAL archeological site near Baghdad, the ruins had been found of a great university, where mathematics, sciences, law, the arts and religion were studied 4,000 years ago.

Mathematics was already a highly developed subject in this part of the country and, 1,400 years before the Greeks, the Babylonians knew all the foundations of classical mathematics. Many problems in algebra and geometry have been found, written on clay tablets. Some only state the exercises but others gave the solutions to the problems and showed the step by step methods used.

There were libraries for keeping written texts together; the texts were usually transcribed in cuneiform (or wedge-shaped) characters.

On the TELL MARDIKH site in Northern Syria, the ruins of a 4,500 years old library have been discovered. It had more than 16,000 tablets containing commercial, administrative, legal, historical and literary texts and also the beginnings of dictionaries.

Writing has not ceased to evolve from that time until this, along with schools, universities, colleges and libraries, whose job is to pass on knowledge and discoveries from one generation to the next. Our culture today would never have existed had it not been for the discoveries of those men thousands of years ago.

Tablet found at Tell Harmal showing a mathematical problem and solution relating to a right-angle triangle.

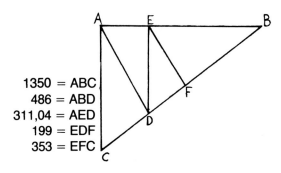

1350 = ABC
486 = ABD
311,04 = AED
199 = EDF
353 = EFC

Egyptian hieroglyphic.

Ancient Egyptian writing.

Ancient Greek characters.

This is a drawing of the "Rosetta stone" where the same text is engraved in three different scripts. This is what helped Champollion, a French historian and linguist, to translate the Egyptian hieroglyphics. It dates from 196 B.C. and was discovered in 1795, in Egypt.

Deciphering ancient writings is a fascinating and difficult subject. Even though many scholars have worked on this, there are still some writings which have kept their secret.

20

today

Today, although there are many localised forms of writing which remain in use, five main handwritings dominate the world. As you can see from the map on pages 24 and 25, these main writing "families" do not coincide with boundaries of language or country. It is interesting to note that they tend to cover vast zones of civilisation, and in particular they reflect the influences of the great religions, each based on a Sacred Book.

The five main writing "families" are described below and to illustrate each of them there follows a story from each civilisation in turn.

Chinese writing is the only non-alphabetic writing still in use. Each ideogram represents an idea or a word. This is made possible by a feature peculiar to the Chinese language, that each word is only one syllable. As each sign stands for an idea, and not for a sound, people knowing other languages can read and understand Chinese, provided that they know the list of ideograms (in the same way that someone who has studied mathematics can understand an equation).

Like all writings which have accompanied a precocious and very brilliant cultural development, Chinese writing has evolved very little although it has been simplified on several occasions. It is bound by numerous literary, and above all religious, texts and is used today by almost one-fifth of the world's population.

Latin writing was derived without a doubt from the Greek alphabet and appeared first about 2,600 years ago. It forms the base of a great variety of languages and is currently the most used writing in the world. It continues to expand and develop.

Indian writing, or rather, writings of an Indian type, is about 2,300 years old. Its origins are unclear but it appears to have borrowed signs from the Phoenician alphabet.

Arab writing uses only consonants. However vowels are indicated by signs placed over or under the consonants. The Arab alphabet was also adopted by Moslem races speaking languages other than Arabic. It is typically a writing covering a zone of influence of a Sacred Book, in this case the Koran, and conveys a particularly rich literature. The first known inscriptions go back about 1,500 years, but before the appearance of Islam.

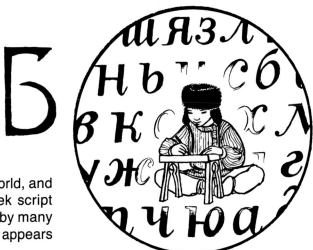

Cyrillic writing is the most recent of the great writings of the world, and is approximately 1,000 years old. It closely resembles Greek script which belongs to a much older family. Cyrillic writing is used by many Slav people. (Greek script is still currently used in Greece — it appears to be the first writing to have invented the use of vowels.)

The invention of writing is a major phenomenon in the history of mankind. It enables thought and discovery of all kinds to cross time and space. By preserving and passing on knowledge it is an indispensable part of progress.

Writing was born in cities and organised states among people whose evolution was accelerating them into societies ahead of their time and who needed to be able to communicate.

What will be the future evolution of writing? Will it be supplanted by other means of preserving and handing down language, such as records or magnetic tapes? Or will there one day be a universal script for everyone?

Whatever the future holds, it is important that writing continues to make communication between races and peoples of different cultures ever more possible and enable them to have an increasing understanding of each other.

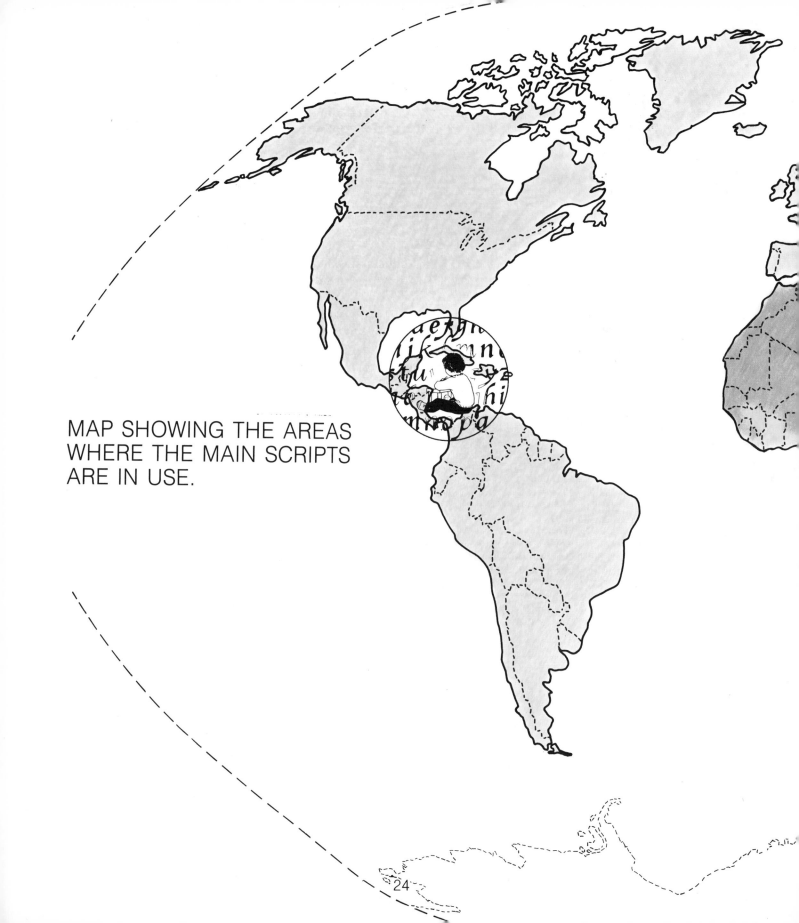

MAP SHOWING THE AREAS
WHERE THE MAIN SCRIPTS
ARE IN USE.

24

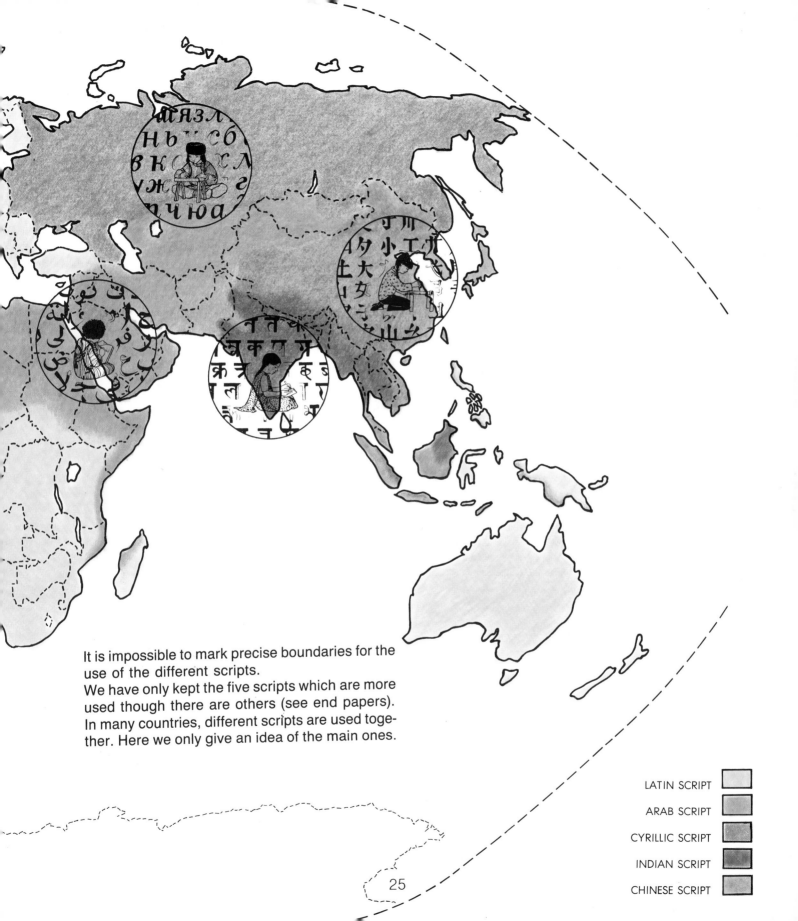

It is impossible to mark precise boundaries for the use of the different scripts.
We have only kept the five scripts which are more used though there are others (see end papers).
In many countries, different scripts are used together. Here we only give an idea of the main ones.

LATIN SCRIPT
ARAB SCRIPT
CYRILLIC SCRIPT
INDIAN SCRIPT
CHINESE SCRIPT

26

A CHINESE TALE

the silken beard

她的家很窮，所以她每天到山上去斬柴。

28

Once upon a time there was a little girl called Huigu. When she was still very young, her father died and as her mother had no other children, Huigu had neither a father, brother nor sister.

Huigu was a pretty child who enjoyed working with her hands. She was very quick and neat and as soon as she had finished one thing, she began another. Everything in the house was beautifully tidy.

29

於是，她更向森林裏跑，想找一個地方躲藏。不一會，她看見樹林後面有一間小屋。

As they were extremely poor she used to go up into the mountains each day to cut wood. By selling the wood, she was able to make enough money to feed her mother and herself and they lived modestly and peacefully.

One day she went out with a shoulder-yoke and ropes to cut wood as usual. She had no sooner entered the forest when torrential rain began to fall. Huigu stood under a huge, thick leaved tree, which at first protected her from the rain, but the downpour was so heavy that soon cold drops were running down her neck. She was wearing nothing but an old worn out shirt which gave no protection against the weather so she decided to go deeper into the forest to find shelter. Suddenly Huigu saw a tiny log cabin, hidden in the trees. She ran towards it, opened the door and went inside.

In the little cabin stood a table, a chair and a bed. There was food on the sideboard, but nobody in sight. Huigu was very tired and hungry too. She put out her hand to take something to eat off the sideboard, but quickly drew it back.

"I have already taken shelter in someone else's house without asking — I'm not going to eat their dinner too."

As she looked around her, Huigu noticed that the floor was dirty and that the table was covered with dust. She took a broom and swept the room until it was neat and clean. Suddenly, a very tiny old man, no more than two feet tall, came in. He had a long white beard down to the ground. When he saw that the room was spick and span, he looked pleased and asked Huigu:

"Did you tidy this room?"

"Yes, I did!" answered Huigu.

"Why did you come here?" asked the little old man.

那個老人從碗櫥中拿出了幾盆菜來招待慧姑，這些菜，她從來沒吃過、甚至不曉得它們的名字。

32

"I came in from the rain. I was so cold and hungry and there was nowhere to shelter. Dear old man, please take pity on me. Allow me to stay here for just one night!"

The old man replied:

"You are a hardworking, intelligent girl. I like you. You may take shelter here."

He took plates of food from the kitchen and set them before Huigu. She had never tasted such delicacies, or even heard their names before, but she found them all sweet and delicious. As soon as she had finished, she fell fast asleep. The old man gently covered her with an eiderdown. Huigu slept heavily until dawn, when she was awakened by the song of birds in the forest.

The old man offered her more delicious food. After the meal, Huigu noticed that his beard was really much too long and, thinking that it must be rather a nuisance for him, she said:

"Dear old man, your beard is much too long. It's not very practical. Shall I cut it for you?"

The old man looked laughingly at his beard and said, "All right, if you like."

Just as Huigu was about to throw away all the strands of beard she had cut off, the old man stopped her and said, "This is a priceless treasure. It must not be thrown away."

Huigu collected all the cuttings and packed them into a handkerchief and handed it to the old man.

The sun was well up when Huigu was ready to go home and reassure her worried mother that she was safe. She said goodbye to the old man.

"I hate to see you leave," he said, "but you must go home. I would like to give you a present so take with you the cuttings from my beard."

He gave Huigu the little parcel. She couldn't help wondering what on earth she would do with it. Seeing her hesitate, the old man said:

她把它們放在織布機上，就織出了一條又亮又細的錦帶。這條絲，一直沒完，也不會折斷。

34

"Don't worry whether it is a useful present or not. You will reap its benefits later."

Huigu thanked him and took the parcel with her. When she got home, Huigu told her mother everything that had happened. Her mother asked to see the beard cuttings. Huigu opened up the handkerchief only to find that the hairs had become long strands of silk.

Huigu's mother put them on her hand-loom and wove a long band of shiny, fine brocade. The thread was never-ending and unbreakable. Huigu and her mother took their work to market and everybody agreed it was the most beautiful silk to be found. They all wanted to buy a piece.

From that day onwards, Huigu made her living by weaving silk brocades and became famous throughout the country.

People called her silk work "threads of light" because of their ever-changing colours and as long as Huigu lived, they never came to an end.

A RUSSIAN TALE

БАБА ЯГА

baba-yaga

Жил да был один старик вдовец
и решил он жениться вторично.
Была у него дочка от первой
жены, тихая и ласковая.

Once upon a time, there was an old man whose wife died and he married again. He had a dear little daughter by his first wife, but her stepmother, who was very beautiful but cruel, hated the child. She beat her and dreamed only of killing her.

Здравствуй тётушка!
Здравствуй родимая,
зачем пожаловала?
Мачеха моя послала меня
к своей сестре Бабе Яге,
спросить нитку с иголкой.

One day, when the father was away, the cruel step-mother said to the little girl, "Go and see your aunt, my sister, and ask her for some needles and thread to make a blouse for you."

This aunt happened to be the ogress, Baba-Yaga, and the little girl, who was no fool, went first to see her other aunt, her own mother's sister.

"Good morning, Auntie!"
"Good morning, my dear. What can I do for you?"
"My stepmother has sent me to see her sister, Baba-Yaga, for some needles and thread to make me a blouse."

"Be careful, little niece," said her aunt, "listen to me. Baba-Yaga exploits those who work for her, and all those who ask her for help. If you are kind to them, perhaps they will help you to escape the terrible danger. Now, there is a servant there — give her a handkerchief. There is a birch tree which will lash your face — tie a ribbon in its branches. The gates will creak and try to close on you. Pour a little oil on their hinges. The dogs will try to bite you — throw them a roll of bread. The cat will try to scratch you — give him a piece of chicken."

Armed with all this good advice, the little girl set out. After a long walk she reached her aunt's house. Baba-Yaga was indoors, weaving.
"Good morning, Auntie."

"Good morning, my dear."

"Mother sent me to fetch needles and thread to make a blouse for me."

"Very well. Take my place and go on weaving for a while."

The little girl sat down behind the loom. Baba-Yaga whispered to a servant:

Когда Баба Яга вышла, девочка
дала коту кусочек мяса и спрашивает,
как же ей теперь от сюда выбраться.

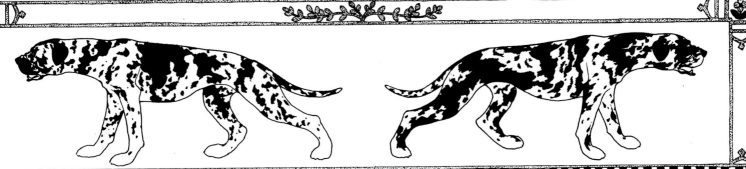

"Quick, heat the bath-water to wash my niece. Take care, because I'm going to eat her for lunch."

The little girl sat still, petrified. Trembling, she asked the servant:

"Why do you obey her?" and she gave her the handkerchief.

After a while, Baba-Yaga came up to the window and asked:

"Are you weaving, little niece? Are you weaving, my dear?"

"I am weaving, Auntie. I am weaving, my dear," replied the little girl and Baba-Yaga went away.

Her terror increasing every moment, the little girl gave the cat a piece of chicken and asked him:

"Is there any way of getting out of here?"

"Take this comb and towel," said the cat, "and go quickly. Baba-Yaga will follow you. Put your ear to the ground and when you hear her approaching, throw down the towel. It will turn into a wide river. If, unluckily, Baba-Yaga manages to cross the river, you must throw down the comb as soon as you hear her footsteps. It will turn into a thick forest, which she will not be able to penetrate."

The little girl took the towel and the comb and ran off as fast as her legs would carry her. The dogs came to bite her, but she threw them the roll of bread, and they let her pass. The gates creaked and tried to close on her, but she poured oil on their hinges and they let her through. The birch-tree tried to lash her face, but she tied a ribbon in its branches and it, too, let her go.

Meanwhile, the cat had taken the little girl's place, but, the more he wove, the more he tangled the threads. Baba-Yaga came up to the window again and asked:

"Are you weaving, little niece? Are you weaving, my dear?"

"I am weaving, Auntie. I am weaving, my dear," replied the cat, softly.

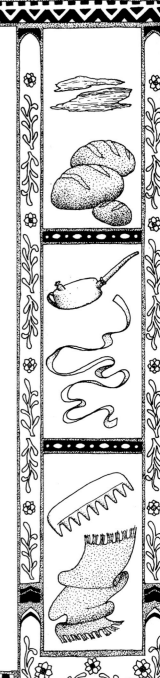

Бросилась Баба Яга от ярости в догоню. А девочка ухо к земле приложила и слушает. Вот уже близко Баба Яга, тогда взяла она полотенце и бросила.

Baba-Yaga rushed into the house and saw that the little girl had gone. She began to scold the cat for not having scratched the child.

"Look how I have served you," replied the cat, "and you've never so much as given me a bone. She gave me a piece of chicken."

Baba-Yaga then furiously attacked the dogs, the gates, the birch-tree and the servant, beating and scolding them.

The dogs said, "Look how we have served you and you have never even thrown us a burnt crust. She gave us a roll of bread."

The gates said, "Look how we have served you and you have never even watered our hinges. She poured oil on them."

The birch-tree said, "Look how I have served you and you have never even tied a piece of string in my branches. She knotted a ribbon among them."

The servant said, "Look how I have worn myself out in your service, and you have never given me a rag. She gave me a handkerchief."

Baba-Yaga was wild with rage. She rushed off in pursuit of the little girl, who put her ear to the ground and heard Baba-Yaga coming. She threw the towel on the ground behind her and it turned into a wide, wide river !

Немного погодя прибежала
девочка домой запыхавшись.
А отец её спрашивает. –
Где ты была? родимая.
Ах батюшка, мачеха посы-
лала меня к своей
сестре Бабе Яге...

When Baba-Yaga found she could not cross the river, she ground her teeth in fury. Quicker than the wind, she tore off home, collected her cattle and brought them to the river. The cattle drank the river dry! Baba-Yaga continued the chase, but the little girl heard her coming once more and threw down the comb. At once it turned into a dark, forbidding forest that chilled one's blood to look at it. Baba-Yaga tried to make her way through it, but, despite all her efforts, she failed and was forced to return home.

When the little girl's father came home, he asked, "Where is my little daughter?"

"She has gone to visit her aunt," said the stepmother.

Just then, the little girl ran in, shaking with fright.

"Where have you been?" asked her father.

"Listen to what happened, father," cried the child. "Stepmother sent me to my aunt to fetch needles and thread to make a blouse for me, and my aunt, Baba-Yaga tried to eat me up!"

"How did you get away, little one?"

"Well," said the little girl, "I was kind to the servant and the cat and the dogs and the gates and the birch-tree and they, in turn, helped me to escape."

When the old man realised what had happened, he looked at his wife with horror. Upset and angry, he sent her away. He kissed his daughter, put the samovar on the hob and they lived happily ever after.

AN ARABIAN TALE

الراعي

the shepherd

خرج **عنترة** وأخوه شيبوب ، ذات يوم ، للبحث عن النوق
العقافير . وهي نوق أسرع في السير من لمح البصر ، ولا توجد الا قرب الحيرة ...

50

One day, Antar set off with his brother, Sheibub, to look for the most fantastic camels.
These could only be found near the town of Hira and were more lively and swift-moving
than a flock of birds.

... تعرِفون عنترة بن الأمير شدّاد ، من قبيلة بني عبس ، وتعرِفون قوة عنترة وشجاعته وكرمه ، وأيّ شاعرٍ هو ، وأيّ مقاتل ، وأيّ فارس عندها يكون على صهوة جوادِهِ الأبجرِ الجميلِ الذي كان يُحبّه حبًّا جَمًّا ...

Maybe you have already met Antar, the son of the emir Sheddad and Zebida of the Beni Abs tribe. You may have heard how handsome he was, how brave and how generous. He was a fine poet, a formidable warrior and a splendid horseman. You may remember, too, how he replied to King Munzir, when he asked him whether or not he was noble.

"My lord, among generous men, the noble one is he who aims his lance, wields his sword and stays his ground in battle. I am doctor to the Beni Abs when they fall ill, I defend them when they are insulted and protect their women when they are attacked. I am the horseman they praise, the sabre that wins victory for them and the poet who sings of their glory."

But this story is not about Antar, it is about his brother, Sheibub. If Antar had been there, things would certainly have been quite different. He would have fought to the death if necessary rather than accept the shepherd's sacrifice...

But listen to what happened.

Antar set out with his brother for Hira, in the direction of Iraq. On their way, Antar hunted while Sheibub drove the wild animals towards him. After riding for several days, they turned off their path to look for an Arab encampment where they could spend the night and find water. Soon they spotted a tent in front of which camels were passing to and fro. An old man came out of the tent and greeted them, his thin body sagged under the weight of his years.

وَإِذَا بِهِمَا يُشْرِفَانِ عَلَى خَيْمَةٍ حَوْلَهَا نِيَاقٌ تِسْعٌ وَجِمَالٌ تَرْعَى. فَخَرَجَ مِنْهَا وَجَاءَ لِمُلَاقَاتِهِمَا

شَيْخٌ أَحْنَاهُ الْكِبَرُ لَمَّا مَرَّتْ عَلَيْهِ مِنَ الْأَيَّامِ وَالسِّنِينَ وَأَنْحَلَتْ جِسْمَهُ اللَّيَالِي فَأَضْحَى سَقِيمًا مَهْزُولًا

...

54

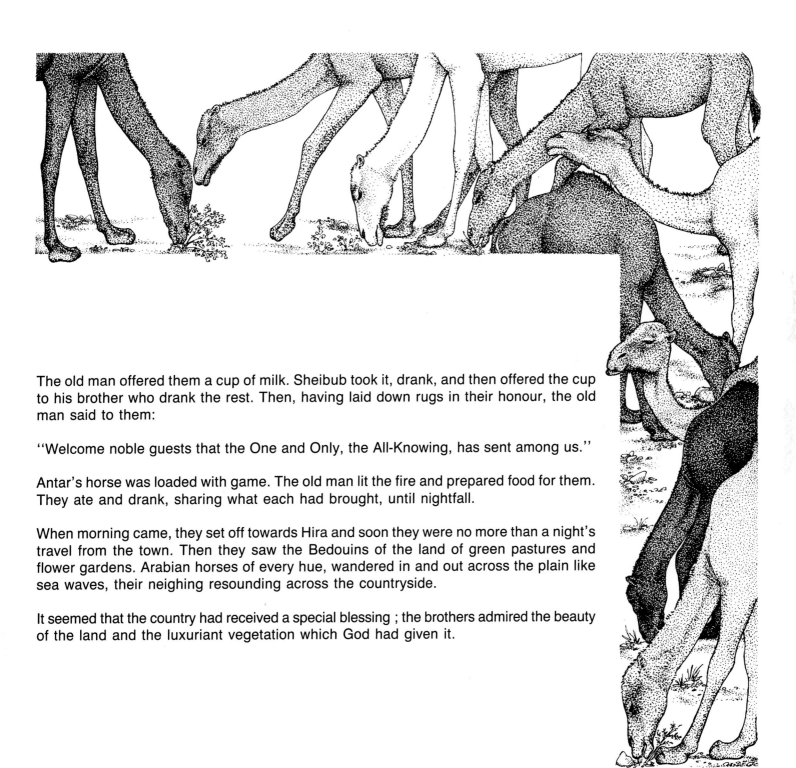

The old man offered them a cup of milk. Sheibub took it, drank, and then offered the cup to his brother who drank the rest. Then, having laid down rugs in their honour, the old man said to them:

"Welcome noble guests that the One and Only, the All-Knowing, has sent among us."

Antar's horse was loaded with game. The old man lit the fire and prepared food for them. They ate and drank, sharing what each had brought, until nightfall.

When morning came, they set off towards Hira and soon they were no more than a night's travel from the town. Then they saw the Bedouins of the land of green pastures and flower gardens. Arabian horses of every hue, wandered in and out across the plain like sea waves, their neighing resounding across the countryside.

It seemed that the country had received a special blessing ; the brothers admired the beauty of the land and the luxuriant vegetation which God had given it.

عنترة وازداد ذهول عندما شاهد الوادي ، أجمل وادٍ رأته عيناه : مياهه فائضة كاللجين المسبوك ، وأشجاره باسقه وثماره وافره وبساتينه رائعة وأزهاره فائحة على جنبات أنهاره الهامسة ، واجتمعت فيه من الطيور الآف تترنم على الأغصان ....

56

There was a valley, the most beautiful Antar had ever seen. Water spilled down like liquid silver. Antar was thrilled by the profusion of trees, the fruits of the palm trees, and the delightful gardens whose murmuring streams were bordered by fragrant flowers. There, thousands of birds sang in the trees, praising God and his creation.

But as usual, many adventures lay in store for our two brothers along the way. So it was one day, Sheibub, thinking his brother had been killed in a battle, fled, his heart filled with deep despair. He was chased by horsemen sent to capture him. Eventually he arrived at the foot of a mountain, in front of a cave. At the entrance he saw a young shepherd with a tanned face. He was roasting a piece of meat in a fire. His sheep grazed in front of him as he prepared his meal.

"Young man," said Sheibub, "please help me. I am in great danger and beg for your protection. Take pity on me, your servant, separated from his brother, and whose enemies are not far off."

"Friend," replied the shepherd, "you have my protection. I would rather die than surrender you to your enemies. Come into my cave, O stranger, and find safety from the hatred of the wicked ones."

... حتى وَصَلَ إلى مَغارة في سَفحِ جَبَلٍ وعلى بَابِها غُلامٌ أسمَرُ اللونِ ، رَاعِي غَنمٍ وامامه نار تشتعل وعليها قطعة من اللحم وهو منهمك في اعداد طعامه ، واغنامه ترعى أمامه ...

58

Sheibub had barely taken refuge in the cave when horsemen drew up in front of the shepherd. They came in groups of ten or twenty.

"Turn him over to us," they cried. "Give us this demon who has disturbed our peace. Make him come out so that we can pierce him with our lances and cut him into pieces with our swords."

"Lords," replied the shepherd, "hear me. Leave him with me. I have given him my word. He has placed himself under my protection and I will not deliver him to his enemies to be killed before my very eyes."

"Come on, come on, bring him out," repeated the horsemen. "If you do not, you will pay for it with your life."

"Noble horsemen," said the shepherd, "if you are intent on forcing me to abandon him, at least grant me this. Move back from the mouth of the cave so that I can release him from my safekeeping. Then it will be a matter between you and him. Kill him but do not destroy my honour, gentle cavaliers, by forcing me to go back on my vow to protect him."

"So be it," they said. "We will do as you wish."

The young shepherd went in to Sheibub.

"Friend," he said, "you have heard what has happened. I no longer know what to think. What's certain is that I am done for. I can only save you at the cost of my own life and that I agree to do with all my heart.

59

... فلبسَ شَيبوبُ ثيابَ الراعي
وَوَضَعَ جُرابَهُ وَزادَهُ على كَتِفِهِ وَأخَذَ عَصاهُ
وَخَرَجَ من المَغارةِ وَقَد أخفاهُ سَوادُ اللَيلِ ...

Take off your clothes and put on mine, then go to them and say: 'I wanted to make the stranger come out of the cave but he refused, so do what you have to with him.' And when you see them setting foot inside here, make a dash to save yourself and leave me with them. I do not fear death. Here is my bag and some food. Go and meet them with this walking stick in your hand. Walk under cover of darkness and I, at least, shall not have to live with the thought that I have betrayed my guest.''

Sheibub put on the shepherd's clothes, hoisted the bag and provisions onto his shoulder, took the walking stick and went out of the cave. The dark night hid him. He spoke to the horsemen as the shepherd had instructed him, and urged the flock forward so as to make his escape, praying to God all the while to save him and the shepherd.

The horsemen rode towards the cave and Sheibub, saved from his enemies, fled into the desert.

The horsemen alighted, entered the cave and brought out the young man. There they recognised the shepherd dressed in Sheibub's clothes. He remained silent, resigned to his death.
"Wretch,'' they cried, "what have you done? Are you so devoted that you will suffer the penalty of death for a stranger?''

فتعجب الفرسان من صنيعه فلم يشاؤوا قتله ولا حتى لومه على إخلاصه . بل عظم في عينيهم فغادروه تاركين أياه ...

"Noble lords," replied the shepherd, "he had sought my protection, and I had given it to him. You came to kill him. I begged you to be merciful and you rejected my prayer. I had no other way of resisting. I have sacrificed my life and I would rather you pierce me with your lances than live, a dishonoured host. If you grant me my freedom, I will be grateful to you until the end of my days. I am a prisoner in your hands, do with me what you will."

The horsemen, filled with admiration for his bravery, had no desire to kill the shepherd, nor to reproach him for keeping his word.

They departed, leaving behind this honourable and brave man, an example of the true sign of nobility that comes from the soul just as Antar had described it to King Munzir.

AN INDIAN TALE

the eclipse of the sun

पास ही के वन से धीमी सी बहती हुई पवन पेड़ों झाड़ियों वनस्पतियों तथा फूलों की भीनी . . . . .

A long, long time ago — days and months and years ago — a peasant couple and their little daughter, Kantra, lived in a village on Mount Aditya.

Kantra was a beautiful child. Her mother watched over her with jealous care, always afraid that her daughter would be kidnapped. But the child's father would say, "Our daughter is a child like any other. She must learn to work and look after the cattle."

The mother obeyed her husband but still had her fears, which turned out to be well-founded.

शेरनी ने कन्त्रा को काड़ी की सेज पर रख दिया और
अपने ही बच्चे की भान्ति उसकी देखभाल की ।।...

One day when a light breeze wafted over, bringing the delicate odour of trees and flowering shrubs and sweet grasses from the nearby jungle, Kantra went to the well to draw water. Yajna, the tigress, lay watching her. With a pounce, she leaped from the jungle, lifted little Kantra in her jaws and carried her away to her lair.

Kantra's poor mother screamed for help and all the villagers chased after the tigress. But they soon lost her tracks amidst the dense undergrowth of the jungle and returned home in the evening in despair.

The tigress laid Kantra on a bed of moss and cared for her as if she were her own child. She brought her the ripest fruit in the jungle. She bathed her in a little lake and, when the nights were chilly, she hugged her in her arms to keep her warm.

So Kantra grew up and every day she became more and more radiantly beautiful.

One day, the other tigers said to Yajna:
"Your daughter has grown big and strong. When are you going to ask us to dinner? She looks ready for eating, we are going to enjoy her good, juicy flesh!"

Yajna made no reply. She waved her tail in the air and ran back to her lair, very worried. Kantra was tidying up and had decorated the entrance with lotus blossoms.

"Kantra, my darling, we are in grave danger. The tigers of my clan are sharpening their teeth to eat you up! We are not strong enough to fight them. You must run far away, and fast!"

Kantra began to cry.

"Where can I go? My parents must be dead now and I know no one else."

"You have only one hope, my darling child," replied Yajna. "You must find the wizard, Vinrou, who lives in the marshes on the other side of the jungle. Only he will know how to hide you. He looks like an enormous toad. I shall try to take you to him."

Off they went at great speed, but they hadn't covered half the ground before they heard the roaring of tigers in the distance.

कन्त्रा कांपती हुई दलदले पानी में
सींकों को पकड़ते हुरे आगे बढ़ी।
ऐसे करके वह ऐक बहुत बड़े मैंडक
के सामने पहुन्ची जो कि एक ...

"We must hurry," said Yajna. "The tigers have realized that we have gone. They are coming to eat you up."

Despite all their efforts, the roaring of the tigers drew nearer and nearer.

"My poor dear," said Yajna, "we must separate. Go straight ahead and when you come to the tallest tree in the jungle, the one with a single enormous flower, turn to the left. I shall stay here and try to hold the tigers back. Think of me when you are in trouble. May the Gods grant you all possible happiness."

Tearfully, Kantra went on alone and Yajna, resigned, lay down to wait. When the tigers arrived, they were furious at losing their prey and the splendid meal they had been looking forward to. In revenge they turned on brave Yajna and savagely tore her to pieces.

Kantra, still in tears, had by this time reached the highest tree in the jungle with a single, enormous flower. She turned to the left and found herself in the marshlands.

Mud oozed up between the grasses and bulrushes and a thick mist hung just above the waters.

Trembling like a leaf, Kantra waded into the bog, holding on to the rushes. Suddenly, she found herself face to face with a huge toad, sitting on a block of crystal. This was the wizard, Vinrou, the Lord of the Marshes.

"Who are you?" he asked, "and, what are you looking for?"

The wizard carefully scrutinised her. Then he said, "Take this toad-skin and put it on. No one will recognize you, but be careful never to take it off, or you will be severely punished. From now on, you will live with me. You will be my servant and I shall protect you from any danger which threatens you."

The toad-wizard was very pleased that chance had brought him such a handsome servant.

Time passed. Kantra was not happy at all. Every day she dreamed of running away, but she couldn't think of anywhere to go.

दौड़ती दौड़ती वह एक ही फूल वाले
पेड़ तक पहुँच कर उस पर चढ़ती
गई थकी हुई अपर पहुँच कर ...

Her only consolation was that she had found a friend in the marshes, a young toad, who was the great-great-granddaughter of the wizard, Vinrou. Kantra recounted her story. She told her that she wanted to run away but did not know how to. She didn't dare go back to humans and if she went back to the jungle, the tigers would eat her up.

The young toadling was sorry for Kantra.
"I shall help you," she said. "Do you remember the very tall tree with a single flower that you passed when you came here? If you don't get dizzy and if you can climb right up to the tree-top and repeat the magic formula that I shall teach you, the tree will grow and grow until it reaches heaven. You can then jump off the tree and stay on in heaven and settle down there."

Kantra felt afraid.

"What is the magic formula?" she asked.

The toadling whispered in her ear:
"Even the birds in their flight,
O Tree, have never attained your kingdom.
Only you know where the stars go in the daytime.
Only you follow the flight of birds in space.
Only you understand the voice of the wind, in all its depths and riches.
Place me, O Tree, on the Path of the Sun."

Kantra thanked the great-great-granddaughter sincerely and, still wearing her toad-skin, she left the marshes.

She ran and ran. When she came to the tree with a single flower, she began to climb — and climb and climb. At the top, she sank back exhausted in the heart of the single flower and whispered:

"Even the birds in their flight,
O Tree, have never attained your kingdom.
Only you know where the stars go in the daytime.
Only you follow the flight of birds in space.
Only you understand the voice of the wind, in all its depths and riches.
Place me, O Tree, on the Path of the Sun."

The flower closed over her, imprisoning her in its white petals and the tree began to grow. It grew so high that it reached heaven. Slowly, the flower opened, and Kantra,

उसने उसे महल का द्वारपाल लगा दिया और उसके रहने के लिये उसे एक छोटे से मकान में बसा दिया।

74

her toad-skin all dusty with golden pollen, climbed down from the flower. The tree gradually returned to its normal size and Kantra stayed on in heaven.

Kantra wandered about for a long time looking for someone to employ her, but no heavenly person would take an ugly toad into his service. The Queen of the Sun at last took pity on the poor toad and put her in a little house as guardian of the Palace gates.

Kantra was happy and she did everything as well as she possibly could. She was no longer afraid of the wizard and sometimes, when she was alone, she took off her toad-skin and gazed at herself in the waters of the lakes. One fine evening, the Prince of the Sun by chance saw her by the lake. He was amazed by her beauty, and told his mother of his discovery. The Queen of the Sun called for Kantra and ordered her to take off the toad-skin. She found her so dazzling that she decided immediately to marry her to the Prince.

After the wedding, the Queen Mother threw the toad-skin into the fire and the lovely young bride began a new and happy life with the Prince of the Sun.

Meanwhile, the toad-wizard had been in a state of fury over Kantra's escape. When he discovered that she was living in heaven and was the wife of the Prince of the Sun, he grew angrier still. The marshes became covered with scum and foul vapours filled the air.

Nearly mad with rage, the wizard climbed to the top of the magic tree and leaped into heaven, intending to devour the Queen of the Sun. The Queen defended herself by shooting sun-arrows at him. The people on Earth, living on Mount Aditya, feared for her safety.

वे मिलकर शंख खड़ताल बरतन घप्पे इत्यादि जिनसे
भी शोर मचा सकते ये लेकर इकट्ठे हुए और अपने
पूरे जोर से उन्होंने ऊधम मचाना शुरू कर दिया ॥

To help her to conquer the toad-wizard, they all gathered together with bagpipes and cymbals, cauldrons and bells — anything capable of making a tremendous noise — and shouted with all their might.

Vinrou could not bear this terrible din, it gave him a splitting headache. He temporarily abandoned the fight and took refuge in his cave in the depths of the marshlands. His anger did not abate, however, and every so often, in moments of fury, he climbed the tree with the single flower and leaped into heaven to devour the Queen of the Sun. And everytime, the people of Mount Aditya gathered together and made as much noise as possible to scare him away.

At these times the rest of the people on Earth would think that there was an eclipse of the sun, but only the people of Mount Aditya knew the truth...

A CELTIC TALE

Ar Luvet

flash of lightning

E-barz he havell koad, war ar bank, ar hoarig
vihan, Lizig, oa koant ha sioul evel
eul labous e kreiz e gousk.

Ar Luvet is the name of the Luguern's cat, down on Penarparc Farm. Nobody knows where the animal came from! From beginning to end, everything about this cat-story is mysterious; and I shouldn't mention the ''end'' either, because, if Mathuline the Tailor is to be believed, this cat will be alive and kicking when all the rest of us have said ''goodbye'' to this life!

81

Perig oe dihumet gand eun dra bennag digus-
tum e beg e dreid, eun dra dom, gwag.
O hunvreal emaon, eme ar beugel ...

I'll begin at the beginning. One peaceful night in early autumn, Peric was fast asleep in his box-bed beside Per, the tall farmhand who was also his godfather. In the next bed, slept his parents and in the third bed, close to the hearth, were his grandmother and grandfather. His pretty little sister, Lisic, slept like a baby bird in the wooden cot standing on a chest.

Peric was woken by something on his feet, something warm and soft. "I'm dreaming," he thought. One previous night, he had awakened with the idea that he was asleep... he dreamt that he was inside the grandfather-clock, only to find on waking that it was simply Per's heart-beat giving out that dull, rhythmic sound he found so reassuring.

But, what was this strange shape? Did it belong to an animal?

The inside of the bed was as black as an oven and only a thin sliver of moonlight passed through the heart-shaped fastening of the doors.

Peric crawled down to the bottom of the bed, taking care not to wake Per. The intruder turned out to be a smooth, furry little animal, but how on earth had it got in? Box-beds have ceilings to them and when the doors are closed nothing can get in.

Peric whispered through the heart shaped opening:

"Mum, there's a rabbit in my bed."

Mum, awoke immediately, like all mothers do when their children call in the night. She also put her lips against the door fastening of her bed, in this case a tiny window in the shape of a star. Peric could hear her laughing as she said to him:

"Stroke his head. I'm sure it's a cat."

Peric went to investigate.

"Yes, it is a cat," he exclaimed, "I can tell by its pointed ears." He took the purring pussy in his arms and went back to sleep.

The next morning Per's shouts woke up the whole household.

"Where did you find this black devil, Peric? Where does he come from?"

The cat yawned and stretched with great disdain. The whole family voiced their astonishment:

Ar haz a vazaillas hag en em zihourdas, ken diseblant ha tra. Ar famill a-bez a estlamas: " Na treud eo, ha divalo, ha pegen dibrad eo war e dreid ! Pe da vare eo deut aze?

"He's so scrawny; he's so ugly; he's so long-legged! When did he get in?"

Suddenly panic-stricken, Peric's grandmother made the sign of the cross and shook her apron at the cat to make it run away.

"You haven't noticed, his eyes are not the same colour! Send him back to the Devil. He's going to bring us all ill-luck."

It was true that the cat was extraordinary; one of his eyes was rust-coloured and flecked with gold; the other was as blue as a baby's.

Peric, who usually loved to lie in bed, got up and dressed in five minutes. He could tell that things were serious and that he would have to defend his new found friend.

The only thing was, would he be right to do so? For a cat, he was enormous, he was dirty and skinny, with bald patches in his fur. All these defects could have been accepted, had it not been for those weird eyes with their penetrating gaze which made people feel distinctly uneasy.

In a terrible dilemma, Peric chose the only way out! He took the poor, starving cat in his arms, climbed like a squirrel up the ladder in the courtyard and left his friend there in the hay-loft above the stables. Peric went to see him three or four times a day, taking bread, milk or cooked vegetables. The cat was half-starved and accepted everything gratefully.

One day, at the end of the morning, Peric had a fright. He found his cat on the edge of the trap-door, wailing desperately.

An oll a redas beteg ar skeul. Ar foenn oe
stlapet 'barz ar porz ha ledet aman hag ahont.
War briadou'zo oe strinket dour. Tan
flamm on kroget da zevel diwarno.

Thick smoke hung everywhere. He noticed that it was unbearably hot in the hay-loft and he recalled his father's words:

"The hay has been brought in damp. Let's hope it won't ferment!"

Well, it definitely was fermenting and Peric cried out, "Papa, Papa, the hay is burning. My cat is calling for help!"

In a split second, the farmer took in the situation and raised the alarm. Everyone rushed to the ladder; in no time, the hay was tossed down and spread over the courtyard, and the armfuls already catching fire were sprayed with water. The cat had saved the house from burning.

Peric came down from the loft with the cat in his arms. And from that day on, the cat had its own special place at the hearthside and was fed special rations of the top-of-the-milk like the new-born calves!

But I nearly forget to tell you why the cat was called Luvet which means flash of lightning. One day he was snoozing on the cowshed roof; he had a habit of perching at dizzy heights. The family was having its midday meal. Suddenly a dark flash crossed the window-pane. Eveybody looked surprised, thinking it must have been a sparrow-hawk diving on a chicken.

In the courtyard, they found the cat stretched over a weasel whose neck he had just broken with his teeth. He had made a truly enormous leap. Under their breath, the maid-servant and Peric's grandmother talked of magic; and the acrobatic cat kept the name Luvet.

At the beginning of winter, Mathuline the Tailor settled in at the farm, as he did every year for the season. He knew a lot of things and the Luguern's cat interested him considerably.

"On my father's farm," said Mathuline one evening, before they all went to bed, "there was a cat that was certainly older than a man. My father had always known him and my grandfather too... He was soot-black, like this one."

"But," said the farmer incredulously, "a cat doesn't live longer than fifteen or twenty years!"

"That's true," said Mathuline, "if you're speaking of ordinary cats. My cat wasn't an ordinary cat. He was as black as Luvet; he had a few white hairs under his chin and a burned patch on his left front paw." Then Mathuline fell silent, overwhelmed by all the mysteries that are unexplained to man.

War e goazez e korn ar hogn
ar haz a hunvree, braz ha trist, e za-
oulagad o wilc'ha a beb eil, al lagad rouz an dro-mañ, al lagad glaz an
dro all.

The cat lay dreaming in his usual place close to the fire, occasionally winking first his rust-coloured eye, then the blue one. The black, silky depths of his fur seemed to melt into the chimney-black and all that could be seen of him was the flame of his eyes.

Feeling a bit dejected, Peric went over to his friend, caressed his head, lifted his chin and, sure enough, the white hairs were there, shining like silver. Peric looked at his mother and she laughed a little nervously.

"Everybody off to bed," she said. "We've had enough witchcraft for one evening."

Peric was upset. He carefully closed the door of his box-bed. Per was already fast asleep. For a long time, the little boy watched his cat through the heart-shaped aperture. He could see the dancing light of the hot coals reflected in the strange eyes of the motionless animal. Peric snuggled up against his godfather, but he still had difficulty in going to sleep.

The next morning, Peric went up to Mathuline who was sitting sewing on the corn-bin.

"Mathuline," he said, "my cat has white hairs under his chin and a burned patch on his left paw. Perhaps it is your cat who has come to us?"

"No, no. It isn't my cat," said the tailor, "but it's another mascot. He'll stay on as long as the house lasts and then he'll disappear. Don't give him away for all the treasure in the world. He chose you. You've nothing to worry about. Somebody is protecting you but I don't want to say his name."

"What rubbish are you telling the child?" called the farmer, roughly.

"We were chatting about everything and nothing," said Mathuline.

Pa'z an d'ober eun dro d'ar vro e
houlennan bewech ouz e gelou.
Gand va hamaradez koz, war ar
blasennig, em-eus kel deuz ar beajou
braz da zond.

As the days and the years went by, the old people went off to the lands of eternal rest. Per got married and left the farm. The parent's hair began to turn grey and Peric became a handsome young man.

Luvet is still there, with his one rust-coloured eye and his one blue eye and the white hairs under his chin.

Is it the same cat? Peric says so, but it's hard to believe.

When I go to the village, I always ask for news of him. In the little square, my old, old friend keeps me in touch with all the departures: "So-and-so died this winter; so-and-so died in the spring."

"And Luvet?"

"The Lord be Praised, Luvet is fine!"

בְּעֵת הַהִיא נְאֻם־יְהֹוָה אֶהְיֶה לֵאלֹהִים לְכֹל מִשְׁפְּחוֹת יִשְׂרָאֵל
לְעָם: כֹּה אָמַר יְהֹוָה מָצָא חֵן בַּמִּדְבָּר עַם שְׂרִידֵי חָרֶב הָלוֹךְ לְהַרְגִּיעוֹ יִשְׂרָאֵל:
מֵרָחוֹק יְהֹוָה נִרְאָה לִי וְאַהֲבַת עוֹלָם אֲהַבְתִּיךְ עַל־כֵּן מְשַׁכְתִּיךְ חָסֶד: עוֹד אֶבְנֵךְ
וּבְנֵית בְּתוּלַת יִשְׂרָאֵל עוֹד תַּעְדִּי תֻפַּיִךְ וְיָצָאת בִּמְחוֹל מְשַׂחֲקִים: עוֹד תִּטְּעִי
כְרָמִים בְּהָרֵי שֹׁמְרוֹן נָטְעוּ נֹטְעִים וְחִלֵּלוּ: כִּי יֶשׁ־יוֹם קָרְאוּ נֹצְרִים בְּהַר אֶפְרָיִם

Hebrew

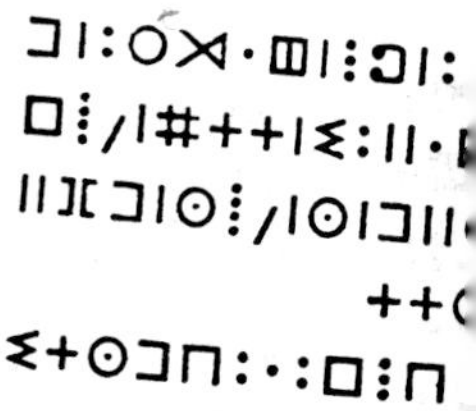

Mayan

አሜን ። ንቀድም ። በረድኤት ።
እግዚአብሔር ። መጽሐፉ ።
ልደቱ ። ለአቡነ ። ቅዱስ ። ተክለ
ሃይማኖት ። ወልደ ። እግዚአብ
ሔር ። በጸጋ ። ወወልደ ። አዳም
በሥጋ ። አዳም ። ወለደ ። ሴት ።
ወሴት ። ወለደ ። ለሄኖስ ። ወሄ

Ethiopian

ΠΝΟΥΤΕ ΠΕΙΩΤ ΟΥΑΓΑΘΟΣ ΠΕ. Ι̅Σ̅ ΠΕΧ̅Σ̅ ΠΧΟΕΙΣ
ΠΕ ΑΥΩ ΠΝΟΥΤΕ. ΟΥΑΓΑΘΟΣ ΠΕ ΠΕΠΝΑ ΕΤΟΥΑΑΒ.
ΠΝΟΥΤΕ ΕΤΕ Μ̅Ν̅ΤϤ ϨΟΥΕΙΤΕ ΟΥΤΕ Μ̅Ν̅ ϨΑΗ ϢΟΟΠ
Ν̅ΤΕϤΜΝ̅ΤΝΟΥΤΕ. Ν̅ΤΟϤ ΓΑΡ ΠΕ ΤΑΡΧΗ ΑΥΩ ΠΧΩΚ

Coptic

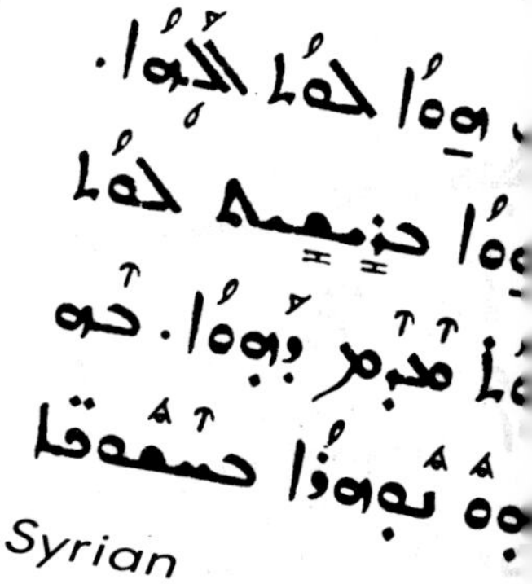

Syrian

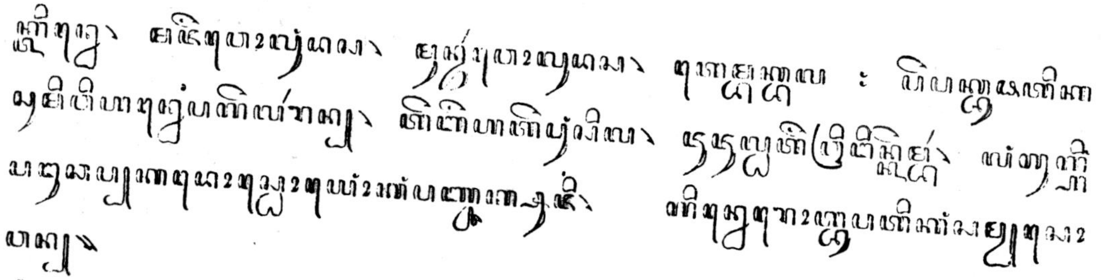

Javenese